...ndship

Is a

Special Gift

Friendship Is a Special Gift

$\mathscr{A}$ friend is a gift whose worth cannot be measured except by the heart.

January 1

*O*ur road will be smooth
  and untroubled
no matter what care life
  may send;
If we travel the pathway
  together,
and walk side by side
  with a friend.

December 31

*W*e cannot tell the precise moment when a friendship starts...it is like filling a vessel drop-by-drop which makes it at last run over; so a series of kindnesses...make the heart run over.

James Boswell

January 2

$\mathscr{I}$f you can help anybody
even a little, be glad; up the
steps of usefulness and
kindness, God will lead
you on to happiness
and friendship.

Maltbie D. Babcock

December 30

*B*lessed are they who have the gift of making friends, for it is one of God's best gifts.

Thomas Hughes

January 3

I know now that the world is not filled with strangers. It is full of other people—waiting only to be spoken to.

Beth Day

December 29

A friend loveth at all times.

Proverbs 17:17 KJV

January 4

*M*any merry Christmases,
many Happy New Years.
unbroken friendships, great
accumulations of cheerful
recollections and affections
on earth, and heaven
for us all.

Charles Dickens

December 28

*F*riends warm you with their presence, trust you with their secrets, and remember you in their prayers.

January 5

$\mathscr{G}$ive generously, for your
gifts will return to you later.
Ecclesiastes 11:1 TLB

December 27

*T*he things that matter the most in this world, they can never be held in our hand.

Gloria Gaither

January 6

I want just one thing. To live long enough to pay back in some way your undeserved and overwhelming generosity.

Pam Brown

December 26

$\mathcal{F}$riendship is the breathing rose, with sweets in every fold.

Oliver Wendell Holmes

January 7

*F*or somehow, not only at Christmas, but all the long year through, the joy you give to others is the joy that comes back to you.

John Greenleaf Whittier

December 25

*O*h, the comfort, the inexpressible comfort, of feeling safe with a person; having neither to weigh thoughts nor measure words, but to pour them all out just as they are.

George Eliot

January 8

*A*gain Christmas: abiding point of return. Set apart by its mystery, mood, and magic, the season seems in a way to stand outside time. All that is dear, that is lasting, renews its hold on us: we are home again.

Elizabeth Bowen

December 24

*W*hen friends meet,
hearts warm.

John Day

January 9

*T*o receive a gift, molded from love and sacrifice, selected with care and tied up with all the excitement the giver has to offer, is indeed rare. They don't come along often, but when they do, cherish them.

Erma Bombeck

December 23

*R*eal friends are those who, when you've made a fool of yourself, don't feel as though you've done a permanent job.

January 10

What brings joy to the heart is not so much the friend's gifts as the friend's love.

Ailred of Rievaulx

December 22

*I*t is not so much our friends' help that helps us as the confident knowledge that they will help us.

Epicurus

January 11

*F*riendship is like two
clocks keeping time.

December 21

I thank my God upon every remembrance of you.

Philippians 1:3 KJV

January 12

A good deed is never lost:
he who sows courtesy
    reaps friendship,
and he who plants kindness
    gathers love.

St. Basil

December 20

*T*he best and most
beautiful things in the world
cannot be seen or even
touched. They must be felt
with the heart.

Helen Keller

January 13

$\mathcal{C}$hristmas is the season for kindling the fire of hospitality in the hall, the genial flame of charity in the heart.

Washington Irving

December 19

When you're with someone
    you trust in,
never needing to pretend,
Someone who helps you
    know yourself...
you know you're with
    a friend.

Amanda Bradley

January 14

A friend hears the song in my heart and sings it to me when my memory fails.

Pioneer Girls Leaders' Handbook

December 18

*W*hen friends ask, there is
no tomorrow...only now.

Alexander Drey

January 15

In whatever [God] does in the course of our lives, He gives us, through the experience, some power to help others.

Elisabeth Elliot

December 17

I wish you long life and happiness—for your long life will be my happiness!

January 16

*B*ear ye one another's burdens.

Galatians 6:2 KJV

December 16

*W*e must love our friends
as true amateurs love
paintings; they have their eyes
perpetually fixed on the fine
parts, and see no others.

Madame d'Epinay

January 17

*H*appiness comes of the capacity to feel deeply, to enjoy simply, to think freely, to risk life, to be needed.

Storm Jameson

December 15

The threads of friendship
embroider our lives with
patterns of joy.

January 18

A friend is one who joyfully sings with you when you are on the mountain top, and silently walks beside you through the valley.

William A. Ward

December 14

*T*here's something beautiful about finding one's innermost thoughts in another.

Oliver Schreiner

January 19

*T*he sun does not shine
for a few trees and flowers,
but for the wide world's joy.

Henry Ward Beecher

December 13

*T*he best mirror is an old friend.

George Herbert

January 20

*N*ow may the warming love
    of friends
Surround you as you go
Down the path of light
    and laughter
Where the happy memories
    grow.

Helen Lowrie Marshall

December 12

$\mathcal{S}$ee to it that you really do love each other warmly, with all your hearts.

1 Peter 1:22 TLB

January 21

*M*ay you wake each day
with God's blessings and sleep
each night in his keeping.

December 11

The friend who is really worth having is the one who will listen to your deepest hurts, and feel they are hers too.

January 22

*T*he heart that has truly loved never forgets.

Thomas Moore

December 10

The person who can make others laugh is blessed.

January 23

A friend never says "I told you so"—even when she did.

Wendy Jean Smith

December 9

$\mathcal{E}$very true friend is a
glimpse of God.

Lucy Larcom

January 24

A merry heart does good, like medicine.

Proverbs 17:22 NKJV

December 8

$\mathcal{D}$o not keep the alabaster boxes of your kindness sealed up until your friends are gone. Speak approving, cheering words while their ears can hear them...and be made happier by them.

George William Childs

January 25

*F*irst keep peace within yourself, then you can also bring peace to others.

Thomas à Kempis

December 7

I can live for two months
on one good compliment.

Mark Twain

January 26

*A*nd all people live, not by reason of any care they have for themselves, but by the love for them that is in other people.

Leo Tolstoy

December 6

$\mathcal{T}$wo lovely berries molded on one stem: So, with two seeming bodies, but one heart.

William Shakespeare

January 27

$\mathcal{L}$ove is a fruit in season at all times, and within the reach of every hand.

Mother Teresa

December 5

*T*he hearts that love will
Know never winter's frost
   and chill,
Summer's warmth is in
   them still.

Eben Eugene Rexford

January 28

$\mathscr{A}$ friend is a present
you give yourself.
Robert Louis Stevenson

$\mathscr{D}ecember$ 4

A word spoken in due season, how good it is!

Proverbs 15:23 KJV

January 29

*W*hat do we live for, if not to make the world less difficult for each other?

George Eliot

December 3

A kind heart is a fountain of gladness, making everything in its vicinity freshen into smiles.

Washington Irving

January 30

*Y*ou are a blessing sent
from Heaven above,
a huggable reminder of
God's unfailing love.

December 2

*W*e have not made
ourselves; we are the gift
of the living God to
one another.

Reine Duell Bethany

January 31

$\mathscr{N}$o love, no friendship can cross the path of our destiny without leaving some mark on it forever.

François Mauriac

$\mathscr{D}$ecember 1

*F*aithful friends are beyond price, and there is no measuring of their goodness.

February 1

I cease not to give thanks
for you, making mention of
you in my prayers.

Ephesians 1:16 KJV

November 30

A friend is the hope of the heart.

Ralph Waldo Emerson

February 2

$\mathcal{O}$ne of the things I keep learning is that the secret of being happy is doing things for other people.

Dick Gregory

November 29

$\mathscr{N}$ever close your lips to those to whom you have opened your heart.

Charles Dickens

February 3

The miles pass more swiftly,
Taken in a joyous stride,
And all the world
  seems brighter
When friends walk by
  our side.

November 28

$\mathcal{F}$riendship is not created by what we give, but more by what we share. It makes a whole world of things easier to bear.

February 4

A good friend remembers
what we were and sees what
we can be.

Janette Oke

November 27

*W*ithout true friends, the world is but a wilderness.

Francis Bacon

February 5

$\mathcal{T}$he best way to cheer
yourself is to try to cheer
somebody else up.

Mark Twain

November 26

*G*od makes our lives
a medley of joy and tears,
hope and help, love and
encouragement.

February 6

A friend is someone who needs me, trusts me, and is happy when my news is good; someone who won't go away.

Angela Douglas

November 25

*I*f you laugh a lot, when you get older your wrinkles will be in the right places.

Andrew Mason

February 7

*L*ove allows us to live,
and through living we
grow in loving.

Evelyn Mandel

November 24

*T*wo are better than one...
for if they fall, the one will
lift up the other.

Ecclesiastes 4:9,10 NRSV

February 8

$\mathcal{O}$f all happinesses, the most charming is that of a firm and gentle friendship.

Seneca

November 23

$\mathcal{T}$here can be no intimacy without conversation. To know and love a friend over the years you must have regular talks.

Alan Loy McGinnis

February 9

A word fitly spoken is like apples of gold in settings of silver.

Proverbs 25:11 NKJV

November 22

$\mathscr{F}$riendship is a cadence
of divine melody melting
through the heart.

Mildmay

February 10

*T*he real art of conversation is not only to say the right thing in the right place but to leave unsaid the wrong thing at the tempting moment.

Dorothy Nevill

November 21

$\mathcal{A}$ joyful heart is life itself, and rejoicing lengthens one's life.

Ecclesiasticus

February 11

*G*od bless the friend
who sees my needs and
reaches out a hand,
who lifts me up, who prays
for me, and helps me
understand.

Amanda Bradley

November 20

*M*ay you always find three
   welcomes in life:
In a garden during summer,
At a fireside during winter,
And whatever the day
   or season,
In the kind eyes of
   a friend.

February 12

*O*ne way to get the most out of life is to look upon it as an adventure.

William Feather

November 19

*T*he real marriage of true minds is for any two people to possess a sense of humor or irony pitched in exactly the same key, so that their joint glances on any subject cross like interarching searchlights.

Edith Wharton

February 13

*W*hat sweetness is left
in life if you take away
friendship? It is like
robbing the world of
the sun.

Cicero

November 18

*O*ur friends are lenses
through which we can better
see ourselves.

February 14

When we dream alone it remains only a dream. When we dream together, it is not just a dream. It is the beginning of reality.

Dom Helder Camara

November 17

*L*aughing at ourselves as
well as with each other gives
a surprising sense of
togetherness.

Hazel C. Lee

February 15

$\mathscr{C}$ontentment is not the fulfillment of what you want, but the realization of how much you already have.

November 16

I have called you friends; because I have made known to you everything that I have heard from my Father.

John 15:15 NRSV

February 16

*T*he best friendships have weathered misunderstandings and trying times. One of the secrets of a good relationship is the ability to accept the storms.

Alan Loy McGinnis

November 15

$\mathscr{F}$riendship is something that raised us almost above humanity.... It is the sort of love one can imagine between angels.

C. S. Lewis

February 17

$\mathcal{D}$ear friends, let us practice loving each other, for love comes from God and those who are loving and kind show that they are the children of God.

1 John 4:7 TLB

November 14

*M*ay God's love guide you
through the special plans
He has for your life.

February 18

$\mathcal{O}$ur job is not to straighten each other out, but to help each other up.

Neva Coyle

November 13

$\mathscr{Y}$our own sky will lighten,
if other skies you brighten
by just being happy
with a heart full of song.

Ripley D. Saunders

February 19

*O*ld friends are the great blessing of one's latter years. Half a word conveys one's meaning. They have a memory for the same events, and have the same mode of thinking.

Horace Walpole

November 12

A friend is a solace in grief and in joy a merry companion.

John Lyly

February 20

$\mathcal{T}$reat your friends as you do your pictures, and place them in their best light.

Jennie Jerome Churchill

November 11

*Y*es, we must ever be friends;
and of all who offer
   you friendship,
let me be ever the first,
   the truest,
the nearest and dearest!

Longfellow

February 21

*W*hen someone does something good, applaud! You will make two people happy.

Samuel Goldwyn

November 10

A good friend will sharpen your character, draw your soul into the light, and challenge your heart to love in a greater way.

February 22

*I*nsomuch as anyone
pushes you nearer to God,
he or she is your friend.

November 9

$\mathcal{T}$here is no joy in life like the joy of sharing.

Billy Graham

February 23

$\mathcal{O}$ne of the best things
people can have up their
sleeves is a funny bone.

Richard L. Weaver II

November 8

$\mathscr{H}$appiness comes to those who are fair to others and are always just and good.

Psalm 106:3 TLB

$\mathscr{F}$ebruary 24

*O*ne does not make friends;
one recognizes them.

Isabel Paterson

November 7

*P*romises may get friends,
but it's performances that
keep them.

Owen Feltham

February 25

$\mathcal{L}$et all of us speak the truth to our neighbors, for we are members of one another.

Ephesians 4:25 NRSV

November 6

$\mathscr{I}$'m so glad you are here....
It helps me to realize how
beautiful my world is.

Rainer Maria Rilke

February 26

*T*here are times when encouragement means such a lot. And a word is enough to convey it.

Grace Stricker Dawson

November 5

I thank God, my friend,
for the blessing you are...
for the joy of your laughter...
the comfort of your prayers...
the warmth of your smile.

February 27

A friend listens to our words but hears our heart.

November 4

*P*eople who deal with life
generously and large-heartedly
go on multiplying relationships to the end.

Arthur Christopher Benson

February 28

$\mathcal{T}$he place where two
friends first met is sacred
to them all through their
friendship, all the more
sacred as their friendship
deepens and grows old.

Phillips Brooks

November 3

A friend is a rare book of which but one copy is made.

February 29

*M*ay you have warm words on a cold evening, a full moon on a dark night, and the road downhill all the way to your door.

Irish Blessing

November 2

$\mathscr{T}$he ornaments of a
house are the friends
who frequent it.

Ralph Waldo Emerson

March 1

*F*riends...they cherish each
other's hopes. They are kind
to each other's dreams.

Henry David Thoreau

November 1

For memory has painted
this perfect day,
with colors that never fade.
And we find at the end of a
perfect day,
the soul of a friend
we've made.

Carrie Jacobs Bond

March 2

*M*oments shared with
you are refreshing streams
of Heaven's Light.

October 31

*M*ay the Lord watch between you and me when we are absent one from another.

Genesis 31:49 NKJV

March 3

$\mathscr{I}$ breathed a song into the air,
it fell to earth I know not where....
And the song, from beginning
   to end,
I found again in the heart
   of a friend.

Longfellow

October 30

$\mathscr{W}$hat wisdom can
you find that is greater
than kindness?

Jean Jacques Rousseau

March 4

*L*ove...keeps no record
of wrongs.

1 Corinthians 13:4,5 NIV

October 29

$\mathscr{N}$othing, so long as I am in my senses, would I match with the joy that a friend may bring.

Horace

$\mathscr{M}$arch 5

$\mathcal{T}$rue friendship comes
when the silence between
two people is comfortable.

Dave Tyson Gentry

October 28

One of the highest
compliments I can receive
is that I am your friend.

March 6

$\mathscr{A}$ true friend is a gift of God...and only He who made hearts can unite them.

October 27

$\mathcal{L}$et not the grass grow on
the path of friendship.

Native American Proverb

March 7

*L*ittle friends may prove
great friends.

Aesop

October 26

I thank you, God in heaven, for friends. When morning wakes, when daytime ends, I have the consciousness of loving hands that touch my own, of tender glance and gentle tone, of thoughts that cheer and bless! Amen.

Margaret Sangster

March 8

*F*avorite people, favorite
  places,
favorite memories of the past...
These are the joys of
  a lifetime...
these are the things
  that last.

October 25

*M*ake new friends
but keep the old.
One is silver
and the other gold.

Joseph Parry

March 9

$\mathcal{T}$here is a grace
of kind listening,
as well as a grace
of kind speaking.

Frederick W. Faber

October 24

The greatest gift we can give one another is rapt attention to one another's existence.

Sue Atchley Ebaugh

March 10

A friend doesn't go on a diet because you are fat. A friend never defends a husband who gets his wife an electric skillet for her birthday. A friend will tell you she saw your old boyfriend—and he's a priest.

Erma Bombeck

October 23

*B*eloved, since God loved us so much, we also ought to love one another.

1 John 4:11 NRSV

March 11

A friend is the one who comes in when the whole world has gone out.

Alban Goodier

October 22

*T*he very possibility of friendship with God transfigures life. This conviction, thus, tends inevitably to deepen every human friendship, to make it vastly more significant.

Henry Churchill King

March 12

*I*f we walk in the light,
as he is in the light, we have
fellowship with one another.

1 John 1:7 NIV

October 21

$\mathscr{I}$t is a fine seasoning for joy to think of those we love.

Molière

March 13

Thoughtfulness is to
friendship what sunshine
is to a garden.

October 20

*T*o have a friend is to have one of the sweetest gifts that life can bring; to be a friend is to have a solemn and tender education of soul from day to day.

Amy Robertson Brown

March 14

*M*ay the road rise to meet you, may the wind be always at your back, may the sun shine warm upon your face, may the rain fall soft upon your fields, and, until we meet again, may God hold you in the palm of His hand.

Irish Blessing

October 19

$\mathcal{F}$riendship is a hug just
when it is needed.

March 15

*W*here your friends are,
there your riches are.

Plautus

October 18

*T*o know someone here or there with whom you feel there is an understanding in spite of distances or thoughts unexpressed—that can make of this earth a garden.

Goethe

March 16

We do not remember days,
we remember moments. Make
moments worth remembering.

October 17

$\mathcal{A}$fter the friendship of God, a friend's affection is the greatest treasure here below.

March 17

*F*riends are necessary to a happy life. When friendship deserts us, we are helpless as a ship left by the tide upon the shore. When friendship returns to us, it's as though the tide came back, giving us buoyancy and freedom.

Harry Emerson Fosdick

October 16

$\mathcal{G}$od shares with the
person that is generous.
Irish Proverb

March 18

$\mathcal{H}$appiness is being at peace; being with loved ones; being comfortable.... But most of all, it's having those loved ones.

Johnny Cash

October 15

*E*ncourage each other
to build each other up.

1 Thessalonians 5:11 TLB

March 19

$\mathscr{F}$riendship is the greatest enrichment I have found.

Adlai Stevenson

October 14

*G*rief can take care of itself, but to get the full value of a joy you must have somebody to divide it with.

Mark Twain

March 20

*F*or God is sheer beauty,
all generous in love, loyal
always and ever.

Psalm 100:5 MSG

October 13

*M*y friends are an oasis to me, encouraging me to go on. They are essential to my well-being.

Dee Brestin

March 21

I always felt that the great high privilege, relief, and comfort of friendship was that one had to explain nothing.

Katherine Mansfield

October 12

A friend is one to whom one may pour out all the contents of one's heart, chaff and grain together, knowing that gentle hands will take and sift it, keep what is worth keeping, and with a breath of kindness, blow the rest away.

George Eliot

March 22

Friends believe in your
dreams as much as you do.

October 11

*W*e don't need soft skies to make friendship a joy to us. What a heavenly thing it is; World without end, truly. I grow warm thinking of it!... Such friends God has given me in this little life of mine!

Celia Thaxter

March 23

A friend is one who incessantly pays us the compliment of expecting from us all the virtues, and who can appreciate them in us.

Henry David Thoreau

October 10

A friendly look,
A kindly smile,
One good act,
And life's worthwhile.

March 24

$\mathcal{D}$o not forget little kindnesses, and do not remember small faults.

Chinese Proverb

October 9

The language of friendship
is not words but meaning.

Henry David Thoreau

March 25

*S*mall service is true service
   while it lasts;
Of friends, however humble,
   scorn not one;
The daisy, by the shadow
   that it casts,
Protects the lingering dew-
   drop from the sun.

William Wordsworth

October 8

A person never gets so rich that she can afford to lose a friend.

March 26

$\mathcal{T}$here is no friend like the old friend who has shared our morning days.

Oliver Wendell Holmes

October 7

$\mathcal{B}$e humble and gentle.
Be patient with each other,
making allowance for each
other's faults because
of your love.

Ephesians 4:2 TLB

March 27

*A*s fire and hearth are inseparable, so are the hearts of faithful friends.

October 6

*F*riendship is like love at its best: not blind but sympathetically all-seeing; a support which does not wait for understanding; an act of faith which does not need, but always has, reason.

Louis Untermeyer

March 28

*P*leasant words are a honeycomb, sweet to the soul and healing.

Proverbs 16:24 NIV

October 5

$\mathcal{T}$here is in friendship
something of all relations, and
something above them all. It
is the golden thread that ties
the hearts of all the world.

John Evelyn

March 29

*L*ife's short and we never have enough time for the hearts of those who travel the way with us. O, be swift to love! Make haste to be kind.

Henri Frédéric Amiel

October 4

$\mathcal{I}$t is our uniqueness that
gives freshness and vitality
to a relationship.

James Dobson

March 30

$\mathcal{O}$ne of life's greatest treasures
is the love that binds hearts
together in friendship.

October 3

$\mathcal{Y}$our best friend is the
person who brings out of you
the best that is within you.

Henry Ford

March 31

*I*n friendship your heart is like a bell struck every time your friend is in trouble.

Henry Ward Beecher

October 2

$\mathcal{T}$he heart that truly loved
never forgets, but truly loves
on to the close.

Thomas Moore

April 1

*O*ther blessings may be taken away, but if we have acquired a good friend by goodness, we have a blessing which improves in value when others fail.

William Ellery Channing

October 1

The true way and the sure way to friendship is through humility—being open to each other, accepting each other just as we are, knowing each other.

Mother Teresa

April 2

We are so very rich if we know just a few people in a way in which we know no others.

Catherine Bramwell-Booth

September 30

$\mathscr{F}$riendship is love with understanding.

Ancient Proverb

April 3

*F*riendship is a word the very sight of which in print makes the heart warm.

Augustine Bell

September 29

*L*ove each other...and
take delight in honoring
each other.

Romans 12:10 TLB

April 4

*W*ise sayings often fall on barren ground; but a kind word is never thrown away.

Arthur Helps

September 28

$\mathcal{T}$here is nothing better
than the encouragement of
a good friend.

Katherine Butler Hathaway

April 5

*M*ost of all, let love
guide your life.

Colossians 3:14 TLB

September 27

I count your friendship one of the chiefest pleasures of my life, a comfort in time of doubt and trouble, a joy in time of prosperity and success, and an inspiration at all times.

Edwin Osgood Grover

April 6

*H*appiness is
my friend's hand.

Gillian Queen, age 10

September 26

*W*hat the dew
is to the flower,
Gentle words are
to the soul.

Polly Rupe

April 7

*K*nowing what to say is not always necessary; just the presence of a caring friend can make a world of difference.

Sheri Curry

September 25

A friend is a person with whom I may be sincere, before whom I may think out loud.

Ralph Waldo Emerson

April 8

*T*here is no surprise more magical than the surprise of being loved. It is the finger of God on [your] shoulder.

Margaret Kennedy

September 24

The great acts of love are done by those who are habitually performing small acts of kindness.

April 9

$\mathcal{G}$od has given us two hands—one for receiving and the other for giving.

Billy Graham

$\mathcal{S}$eptember 23

I thank God far more for friends than for my daily bread—for friendship is the bread of the heart.

Mary Mitford

April 10

$\mathcal{D}$on't walk in front of me,
I may not follow. Don't walk
behind me, I may not lead.
Walk beside me and just be
my friend.

Albert Camus

September 22

$\mathcal{T}$he more we love, the better we are.

Jeremy Taylor

April 11

$\mathcal{R}$ich is the woman who has a praying friend.

Janice Hughes

September 21

$\mathcal{P}$ut on a heart of compassion, kindness, humility, gentleness, and patience.

Colossians 3:12 NAS

April 12

If we had all the riches
that we could ever spend,
it could never buy the
treasures the heart finds
in a friend.

September 20

$\mathcal{T}$he ideal of friendship
is to feel as one while
remaining two.

Madame Swetchine

April 13

$\mathcal{S}$ay only what is good
and helpful to those you
are talking to, and what
will give them a blessing.

Ephesians 4:28 TLB

$\mathcal{S}$eptember 19

If we would build on a
sure foundation in friendship,
we must love our friends
for their sakes rather than
our own.

Charlotte Brontë

April 14

*W*hat the heart gives away
   is never gone...
It is kept in the hearts
   of others.

Robin St. John

September 18

A friend is a close
companion on rainy days,
someone to share with through
every phase...
Forgiving and helping to bring
out the best,
believing the good
and forgetting
the rest.

April 15

*T*rue friends, like ivy
and the wall,
Both stand together,
and together fall.

September 17

A friend is someone who laughs at your jokes when they're not very funny and sympathizes with your problems when they're not very serious.

April 16

Friendship: Gentle as the dew from silken skies, radiant as some glorious diadem, set with countless stars.

Yeoman Shield

September 16

*I*n tight places one's friends are apparent.

Petronius

April 17

$\mathscr{A}$ true friend is of more price than a kingdom.

John Lyly

September 15

*A*s o'er the glacier's
frozen sheet
Breathes soft the Alpine rose,
So, through life's desert
springing sweet,
The flower of friendship
grows.

Oliver Wendell Holmes

April 18

*W*e have been friends
together, in sunshine
and in shade.

Caroline Norton

September 14

*A*mong God's best gifts to
us are the people who love us.

April 19

*M*y friends have made the story of my life. In a thousand ways they have turned my limitations into beautiful privileges, and enabled me to walk serene and happy in the shadow cast by my deprivation.

Helen Keller

September 13

*B*e kind to one another, tenderhearted, forgiving one another, as God in Christ has forgiven you.

Ephesians 4:32 NRSV

April 20

$\mathcal{T}$he world is a rose:
smell it and pass it on
to your friends.

Persian Proverb

September 12

$\mathscr{A}$s a countenance is made
beautiful by the soul's shining
through it, so the world is
beautiful by the shining
through it of God.

Friedrich Heinrich Jacobi

April 21

And whatever you do, do it with kindness and love.

1 Corinthians 16:14 TLB

September 11

$\mathcal{F}$riendship is not won by
the giving of things, but by
the giving of the heart.

Roy Lessin

April 22

He who gives in
friendship's name shall
reap what he has spent.

Anne S. Eaton

September 10

$\mathcal{A}$ cup of tea, a prayer
or two,
blessed moments shared
with you.

Ellen Cuomo

April 23

*H*is thoughts were slow,
His words were few,
  and never formed to glisten,
But he was a joy to all
   his friends—
You should have heard
   him listen.

quoted by Wayne Mackey

September 9

$\mathcal{L}$ife is fortified by many friendships. To love, and to be loved, is the greatest happiness of existence.

Sydney Smith

April 24

$\mathcal{O}$ur friends see the best in us, and by that very fact call forth the best from us.

Hugh Black

September 8

I wish you all the joy that you can wish.

Shakespeare

April 25

"*Stay*" is a charming word
in a friend's vocabulary.

Amos Bronson Alcott

September 7

A friend is dearer than the light of heaven; for it would be better for us that the sun were extinguished, than that we should be without friends.

Chrysostom

April 26

*E*ach of us has something different to contribute, and no matter how small or insignificant it may seem, it can be for the benefit of all.

Lauritz Melchior

September 6

There is no better exercise
for the heart than reaching
down and lifting up people.

John Andrew Holmer

April 27

*F*riendships begun in this world can be taken up again in heaven, never to be broken off.

Francis de Sales

September 5

$\mathcal{D}$o to others as you would
have them do to you.

Luke 6:31 NRSV

April 28

*M*ay happiness touch your life today as warmly as you have touched the lives of others.

September 4

*F*riends...lift our spirits, keep us honest, stick with us when times are tough, and make mundane tasks enjoyable. No wonder we want to make friends.

Em Griffin

April 29

Whenever we can we should always be kind to everyone.

Galatians 6:10 TLB

September 3

$\mathcal{T}$hey are rich who have true friends.

Thomas Fuller

April 30

$\mathcal{T}$he road to a friend's
house is never long.

Danish Proverb

September 2

$\mathcal{T}$he uncertainties of the present always give way to the enchanted possibilities of the future.

Kirkland

May 1

*F*riendship: It involves many things, but, above all, the power of going out of one's self and seeing and appreciating whatever is noble and loving in another.

Thomas Hughes

September 1

*T*hose who bring sunshine
to the lives of others cannot
keep it from themselves.

James M. Barrie

May 2

*H*e does good to himself
who does good to his friends.

Erasmus

August 31

My friend is not perfect—
no more than I am—and so
we suit each other admirably.
Alexander Smith

May 3

*W*hat lies behind us, and what lies before us are tiny matters, compared to what lies within us.

Ralph Waldo Emerson

August 30

$\mathscr{A}$ friend is what the heart
needs all the time.

Henry van Dyke

May 4

A friend is a person with whom you dare to be honest.

Frank Crane

August 29

*F*ew delights can equal the mere presence of one whom we trust utterly.

George MacDonald

May 5

They are closest to us who best understand what life means to us, who feel for us as we feel for ourselves, who are bound to us in triumph and disaster, who break the spell of our loneliness.

Henry Alonzo Myers

August 28

$\mathscr{T}$hrough love serve one another.

Galatians 5:13 KJV

May 6

*N*othing but heaven itself
is better than a friend who is
really a friend.

Plautus

August 27

$\mathcal{F}$riendship is one of the sweetest joys of life.

Charles H. Spurgeon

May 7

*B*e perfect, be of good
comfort, be of one mind,
live in peace; and the God
of peace shall be with you.

2 Corinthians 13:11 KJV

August 26

*F*riendship is a gift
from God
that's blessed in every part...
born through love
and loyalty...
conceived within
the heart.

May 8

*F*riendship is sharing
openly, laughing often,
trusting always,
caring deeply.

August 25

*T*he light of friendship
is...seen plainest when all
around is dark.

Cromwell

May 9

*J*oy descends gently upon us like the evening dew, and does not patter down like a hailstorm.

Jean Paul Richter

August 24

A faithful friend is a strong defense: and he that hath found such a one hath found a treasure.

Ecclesiasticus

May 10

*K*indness opens in each heart a little heaven.

August 23

*I*t is an awesome, challenging thought: The Lord comes to us in our friends. What we do and are to them is an expression of what we are to Him.

Lloyd John Ogilvie

May 11

$\mathscr{F}$riendship is not diminished
by distance or time,...by
suffering or silence. It is in
these things that it roots
most deeply. It is from these
things that it flowers.

Pam Brown

August 22

*T*rue friends are like good books. You don't always use them, but you know where they are when you need them.

May 12

$\mathcal{F}$rom the simple seeds
of understanding, we reap
the lovely harvest of
true friendship.

August 21

Friendship is a flower that blossoms in the heart.

May 13

*I*n good times and bad,
we need friends who will
pray for us, listen to us, and
lend a comforting hand
and an understanding ear
when needed.

Beverly LaHaye

August 20

There are "friends" who pretend to be friends, but there is a friend who sticks closer than a brother.

Proverbs 18:24 TLB

May 14

*F*riendship is a cozy shelter
from life's rainy days.

August 19

And of all best things
upon the earth, I hold that a
faithful friend is the best.

Edward Bulwer-Lytton

May 15

*L*et each esteem the other better than themselves.

Philippians 2:3 KJV

August 18

A smile is the lighting system of the face and the heating system of the heart.

Barbara Johnson

May 16

*I*t is easy to say how we love new friends, and what we think of them, but words can never trace out all the fibers that knit us to the old.

George Eliot

August 17

A pleasant companion
reduces the length of a
journey.

Syrus

May 17

*A*ll our actions take their hue from the complexion of the heart, as landscapes their variety from light.

Francis Bacon

August 16

*F*riendship is precious, not only in the shade, but in the sunshine of life; and thanks to a benevolent arrangement of things, the greater part of life is sunshine.

Thomas Jefferson

May 18

$\mathcal{H}$elping and serving in a friendship seals our need for each other and gives us a sense of personal fulfillment and satisfaction.

Jerry and Mary White

August 15

*W*ishing to be friends is
quick work, but friendship
is a slow ripening fruit.

Aristotle

May 19

A friend is one who believes in you before you believe in yourself.

August 14

*T*he best gifts are tied
with heartstrings.

May 20

*T*he healthiest relationships are those that breathe—that move out and then move back together.

James Dobson

August 13

*F*riendship, like the immortality of the soul, is too good to be believed. When friendships are real, they are not glass threads or frostwork, but the solidest things we know.

Ralph Waldo Emerson

May 21

*L*ike ice cream, our
friendship
Has so many flavors!
And some day I hope
to return
All your favors!

August 12

*I*f you love someone you will be loyal to him no matter what the cost.

1 Corinthians 13:7 TLB

May 22

*F*riendships are purer and the more ardent, the nearer they come to the presence of God, the Sun not only of righteousness but of love.

Walter S. Landor

August 11

$\mathscr{T}$rue friends are never
   far apart,
each keeps the other in
   her heart.

May 23

$\mathscr{G}$od is love. Whoever
lives in love lives in God,
and God in him.

1 John 4:16 NIV

August 10

*M*y friend shall forever be my friend, and reflect a ray of God to me.

Henry David Thoreau

May 24

*L*aughter is the shortest distance between two people.

Victor Borge

August 9

$\mathcal{B}$e on the lookout for mercies. The more we look for them, the more of them we will see. Blessings brighten when we count them.

Maltbie D. Babcock

May 25

*F*riendship consists in
forgetting what one gives,
and remembering what
one receives.

Alexandre Dumas

August 8

The happiness of life is made up of minute fractions— the little, soon-forgotten charities of...a kind look or heartfelt compliment.

Samuel Taylor Coleridge

May 26

*T*he memory of childhood
friendships softens the heart.

August 7

The way from God to
a human heart is through
a human heart.

S. D. Gordon

May 27

*E*ncouragement is awesome.
It [can] actually change the
course of another person's
day, week, or life.

Charles R. Swindoll

August 6

*H*old a true friend with both your hands.

Nigerian Proverb

May 28

$\mathcal{T}$he most precious of all possessions is a wise and loyal friend.

Herodotus

August 5

*B*lessed are the ones God sends to show his love for us...our friends.

May 29

$\mathscr{O}$ne friend ever watches
and cares for another.

Randle Cosgrave

August 4

$\mathcal{N}$o one has greater love
than this, to lay down one's
life for one's friends.

John 15:13 NRSV

$\mathcal{W}$hat a blessing is a friend
with a heart so trustworthy that
you may safely bury all your
secrets in it, who can relieve your
cares by her words, your doubts
by her advice, your sadness
by her good humor, and
whose very look gives
comfort to you.

August 3

A true friend calls out growth in the other person. Of course, you can't make anyone grow, but being a friend means you provide the stimulus that will promote growth.

Jim Conway

May 31

*B*e full of sympathy toward each other, loving one another with tender hearts and humble minds.

1 Peter 3:8 TLB

August 2

*A*ll who joy would win
Must share it—happiness
was born a twin.

Byron

June 1

The faithful friend is
beyond price, and there is
no weighing of his goodness.
Book of Wisdom

August 1

*F*riends should be treasured.
And to have good friends, you
must *be* a good friend.

Angela Douglas

June 2

A friend is one who knows all about you and won't go away.

July 31

*S*pontaneity is one of
the great joys of a strong
friendship.

Jerry and Mary White

June 3

$\mathcal{T}$here never was any heart
truly great and generous, that
was not also tender and
compassionate.

Robert South

July 30

*F*riendship makes prosperity brighter, while it lightens adversity by sharing its griefs and anxieties.

Cicero

June 4

*O*ur lives are filled with
   simple joys
and blessings without end,
And one of the greatest joys
   in life
is to have a friend.

July 29

*M*ercy is as beautiful in a time of trouble as rain clouds in a time of drought.

Ecclesiasticus

June 5

*W*hoever has a heart full of love always has something to give.

Pope John XXIII

July 28

$\mathcal{F}$riendship's best fate is when it can spend a life, a fortune, all to serve a friend.

John Bertram Phillips

June 6

*M*ay the hinges of friendship never rust, nor the wings of love lose a feather.

E. B. Ramsey

July 27

$\mathcal{F}$or the whole law is summed up in a single commandment, "You shall love your neighbor as yourself."

Galatians 5:14 NRSV

June 7

*S*ome people are so special
that once they enter your life,
it becomes richer and fuller
and more wonderful than you
ever thought it could be.

July 26

*T*ogether we stick;
divided we're stuck.

Evon Hedly

June 8

$\mathcal{T}$he cheerful heart has
a continual feast.

Proverbs 15:15 NIV

July 25

*Y*ou have done it without a touch. Without a word, without a sign. You have done it by being yourself. Perhaps that is what being a friend is.

Roy Croft

June 9

*B*etter without gold than without a friend.

Cahier

July 24

*I*n friendship's fragrant
    garden,
There are flowers of every hue.
Each with its own fair beauty
And its gift of joy for you.

June 10

*S*o shall a friendship fill
   each heart
With perfume sweet as
   roses are,
That even though we be apart,
We'll scent the fragrance
   from afar.

Georgia McCoy

July 23

*T*rue gratitude, like true love, must find expression in acts, not words.

R. Mildred Barker

June 11

$\mathcal{T}$hank you for the treasure
of your friendship...for
showing me God's special
heart of love.

July 22

There are red-letter days
in our lives when we meet
people who thrill us like a
fine poem.... The influence of
their calm, mellow natures
is a libation poured
upon [us].
Helen Keller

June 12

*T*he supreme happiness of life is the conviction that we are loved, loved for ourselves, or rather loved in spite of ourselves.

Victor Hugo

July 21

*A*ngels from friendship
gather half their joys.

Young

June 13

*F*riendship is a
sheltering tree;
Oh, the joys that come
down shower-like!

Samuel Taylor Coleridge

July 20

$\mathcal{I}$ have learned that to have a good friend is the purest of all God's gifts, for it is a love that has no exchange of payment.

Frances Farmer

June 14

$\mathscr{B}$lessed is the influence of
one true, loving human soul
on another.

George Eliot

July 19

I will never leave you
or forsake you.

Hebrews 13:5 NRSV

June 15

*L*ittle deeds of kindness,
  little words of love,
Help to make earth happy
  like the Heaven above.

Julia F. Carney

July 18

*O*h better than the minting
Of a gold-crowned king
Is the safe-kept memory
Of a lovely thing.

Sara Teasdale

June 16

$\mathcal{B}$lessed are the peace-makers; for they shall be called the children of God.

Matthew 5:9 KJV

July 17

*F*riendship is the poetry
of life.

June 17

$\mathcal{T}$rue happiness consists not in the multitude of friends, but in the worth and the choice.

Ben Jonson

July 16

*Y*our highest pleasure is
that which rebounds from
hearts that you have
made glad.

Henry Ward Beecher

June 18

*L*et there be many
windows in your soul,
That all the glory of the
universe may beautify it.

Ella Wheeler Wilcox

July 15

A knowledge that another has felt as we have felt, and seen things not much otherwise than we have seen them, will continue to the end to be one of life's choicest blessings.

Robert Louis Stevenson

June 19

$\mathcal{F}$riends will not only live
in harmony, but in melody.

Henry David Thoreau

July 14

*I*t is always good to know, if only in passing, a charming human being; it refreshes our lives like flowers and wood and clear brooks.

George Eliot

June 20

$\mathcal{A}$ mile walked with
a friend contains only a
hundred steps.

Russian Proverb

July 13

A friend is a person with a sneaky knack of saying good things about you behind your back.

June 21

*G*enuine friends can enter
into our celebration with as
much or more enthusiasm
as they would have if the
fortuitous serendipity had
happened to them.

Lloyd John Ogilvie

July 12

$\mathcal{G}$od has put something
noble and good into every
heart his hand created.

Mark Twain

June 22

*K*ind words are jewels
that live in the heart and
soul and remain as
blessed memories.

Marvea Johnson

July 11

*S*hare each other's troubles
and problems, and so obey
the Lord's command.

Galatians 6:2 TLB

June 23

$\mathcal{W}$e find happiness, peace,
and heart's content when we
enter the house of a friend.

July 10

*G*ood company on a
journey makes the way
to seem the shorter.

Izaak Walton

June 24

$\mathscr{B}$lessed are the merciful,
for they shall obtain mercy.

Matthew 5:7 KJV

July 9

*A*ttention to detail is the
secret of success in every sphere
of life, and little kindnesses, little
acts of considerateness, little
appreciations, little confidences...
they are all that are needed to
keep the friendship sweet.

Hugh Black

June 25

*Y*ou entered my life in a casual way, and saw at a glance what I needed. There were others who passed me or met me each day, but never a one of them heeded.

Grace Stricker Dawson

July 8

*F*riendship above all ties
does bind the heart,
And faith in friendship
is the noblest part.

Lord Orrery

June 26

*F*lowers leave their
fragrance on the hand
that bestows them.

Chinese Proverb

July 7

$\mathcal{T}$o be able to find joy in another's joy, that is the secret of happiness.

George Bernanos

June 27

*O*ur chief want in life is somebody who shall make us do what we can. This is the service of a friend.

Ralph Waldo Emerson

July 6

*F*riends are the flowers in
the garden of life.

June 28

The most precious of all possessions is a wise and loyal friend.

Darius

July 5

*I*f instead of a gem, or even a flower, we should cast the gift of a loving thought into the heart of a friend, that would be giving as the angels give.

George MacDonald

June 29

*D*o all the good you can
By all the means you can
In all the ways you can
In all the places you can
To all the people you can
As long as ever you can.

John Wesley

July 4

*N*o one is useless in this world who lightens the burdens of it for another.

Charles Dickens

June 30

*N*othing opens the heart like a true friend, to whom you may impart griefs, joys, fears, hopes,...and whatever lieth upon the heart.

Francis Bacon

July 3

*W*hen others are happy, be happy with them. If they are sad, share their sorrow.

Romans 12:15 TLB

July 1

$\mathcal{T}$he older you get the more you realize that kindness is synonymous with happiness.

Lionel Barrymore

July 2